Contents

Words appearing in the text in bold, **like this**, are explained in the Glossary.

 Find out more about Italy at
www.heinemannexplore.co.uk

Where is Italy?

To learn more about Italy we meet three children who live there. Italy is a country in Europe. Italy is surrounded by the Mediterranean Sea.

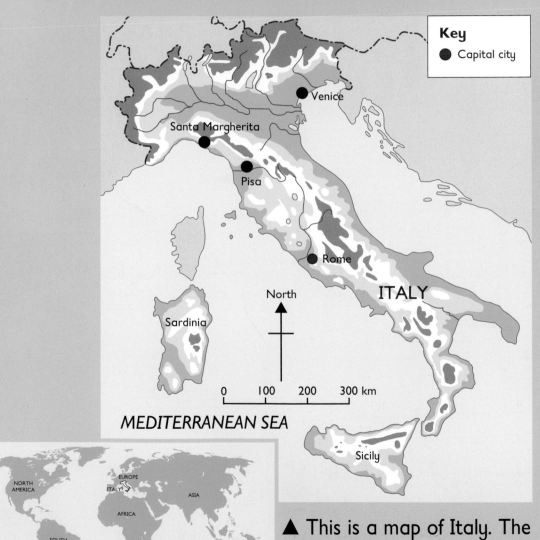

Key
● Capital city

Venice

Santa Margherita

Pisa

Rome

ITALY

North

Sardinia

0   100   200   300 km

MEDITERRANEAN SEA

Sicily

NORTH AMERICA

EUROPE

ITALY

ASIA

AFRICA

SOUTH AMERICA

AUSTRALIA

▲ This is a map of Italy. The capital city of Italy is Rome.

Winters are very cold in the north of Italy. Summers are very hot in the south of Italy. There are **earthquakes** and **volcanoes** in some places in Italy.

Italy has hills and ▶ mountains. It also has flat low land near the sea.

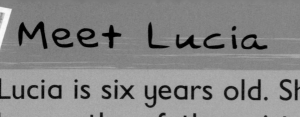

Meet Lucia

Lucia is six years old. She lives with her mother, father, sister and brother. Her family live in a flat in Rome, the capital city of Italy.

Lucia

Lucia's sister

▲ Lucia's father is an **architect**. Her mother is a teacher.

6

▼ Lucia likes eating spaghetti!

Lucia's mother

Lucia's father

Lucia's sister

Lucia

Lucia's family have a meal together in the evening. Lucia helps by setting the table. On special days they eat fish. Lucia prefers eating cottage cheese or ice-cream.

Lucia's day

Lucia goes to school five days a week.
She learns maths, Italian, art, music,
religious education and English.
Lucia likes art because it
is messy!

Lucia's mother

Lucia walks to ▶
school with
her mother.

▲ For a treat,
Lucia is allowed
an ice cream!

After school, Lucia is looked after by
her mother. Sometimes they go for a
walk around Rome. There are lots of
interesting places to visit in Rome.

Playtime

When Lucia is not at school she likes to play. She plays with her brother and sister. The block of flats she lives in has a big, garden to play in.

◀ Lucia likes to go swimming and to ride her bike.

Lucia has lots of friends. She likes to play in the park with her friends. Her best friend is called Adriana. She and Lucia tell each other jokes.

▼ Lucia likes funny friends who make her laugh.

Historic buildings

Italy has a very interesting past. Many tourists visit Italy to see its ancient landmarks. The Colosseum in Rome was built by the Ancient Romans nearly 2000 years ago.

▼ People used to watch **gladiators** fight at the Colosseum.

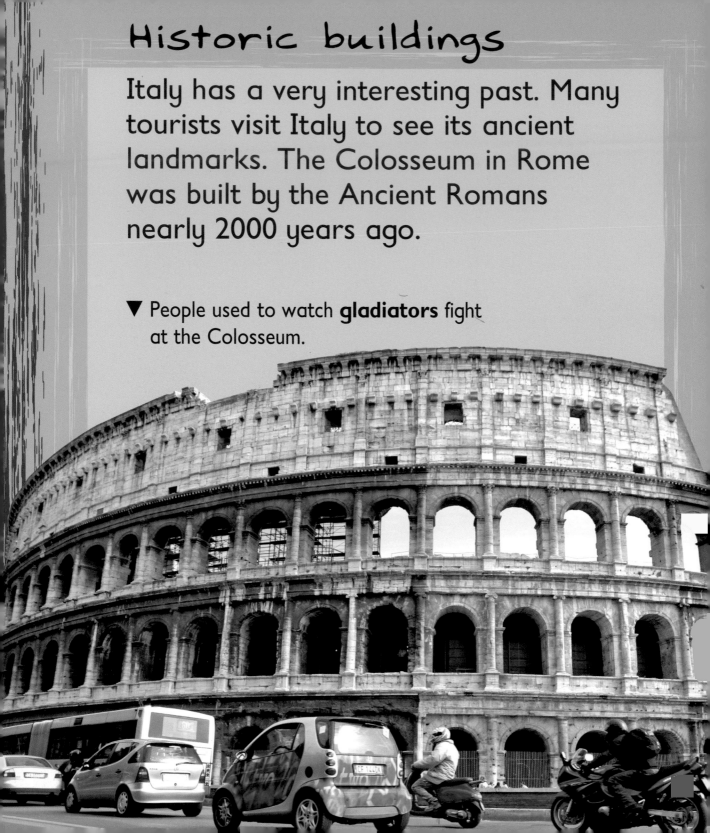

People can walk to the ▶
top of the tower.

The Leaning Tower of Pisa was built about 900 years ago. It took over 200 years to finish. The tower was built straight but now leans to one side!

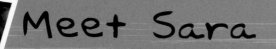

Meet Sara

Sara is seven years old. She lives with her mother, father and sister. Sara and her family live in Venice. Venice is made up of lots of small islands.

▼ There are lots of **canals** running through Venice.

▼ Sara's father has to work at weekends. Her family try to spend time together when he is not working.

Sara's mother

Sara's father

Sara

Sara's sister

There are no cars or buses in Venice. People travel by boat. One boat used in Venice is called a **gondola**. Sara's father takes people around Venice in a gondola.

15

Fun in Venice

Sara goes to school five days a week. After school she plays with her sister and her friends. She likes to read books, skate and ride her bike.

There are no cars in Venice so it is very safe to skate. ▶

Sometimes Sara and her mother and sister visit her father on his **gondola**. He takes them for trips around the city.

▼ Sara's father wears a **traditional** uniform at work.

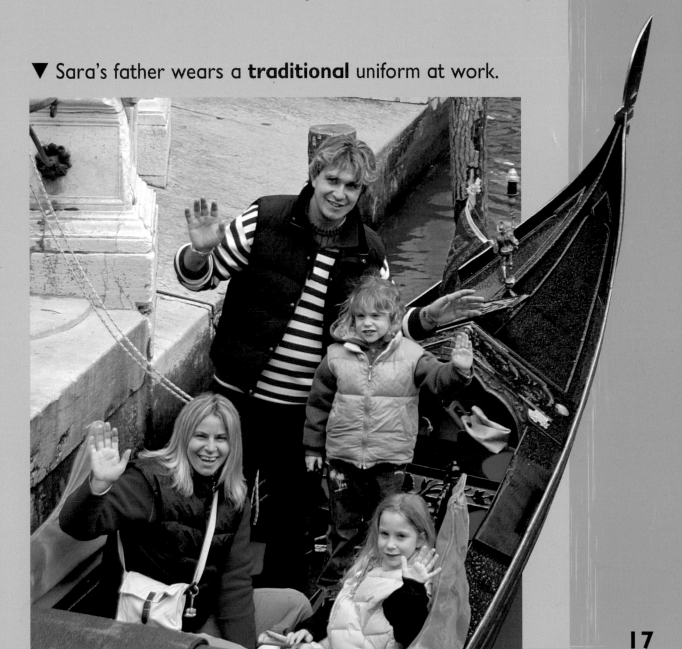

Chocolate!

Venice is famous for its pizza and seafood. Sara likes pizza, but she loves eating chocolate. She enjoys making chocolate spread sandwiches!

▼ Sara's favourite food is chocolate spread!

Sara looks forward to special days and **festivals** in the year. Her favourite time is Easter. She and her sister receive lots of chocolate Easter eggs.

19

Making and growing things

People in Italy make and grow lots of goods to sell around the world. Venice is famous for its masks. People can go and watch them being made.

One of the islands in ▶ Venice is called Murano. Murano is famous for the glass that is made there.

▼ Grapes are grown
in vineyards.

▲ Oranges grow
well in the
south of Italy.

Different foods grow well in different
parts of Italy. Wheat and vines,
olive, fig and orange trees all grow
in Italy. There are also fields full of
colourful sunflowers.

21

Meet Alberto

Alberto is eight years old. He lives with his mother, father and sister in a small town called Santa Margherita. Santa Margherita is near the sea.

◀ Alberto lives a few minutes from the beach.

▼ Alberto's family always eat breakfast together at the weekend.

Alberto

Alberto's mother

Alberto's sister

Alberto's father

Alberto's parents work by helping people who visit Italy on holiday. His father has to work away from home all week. At the weekend the family like to spend time together.

23

Alberto's school

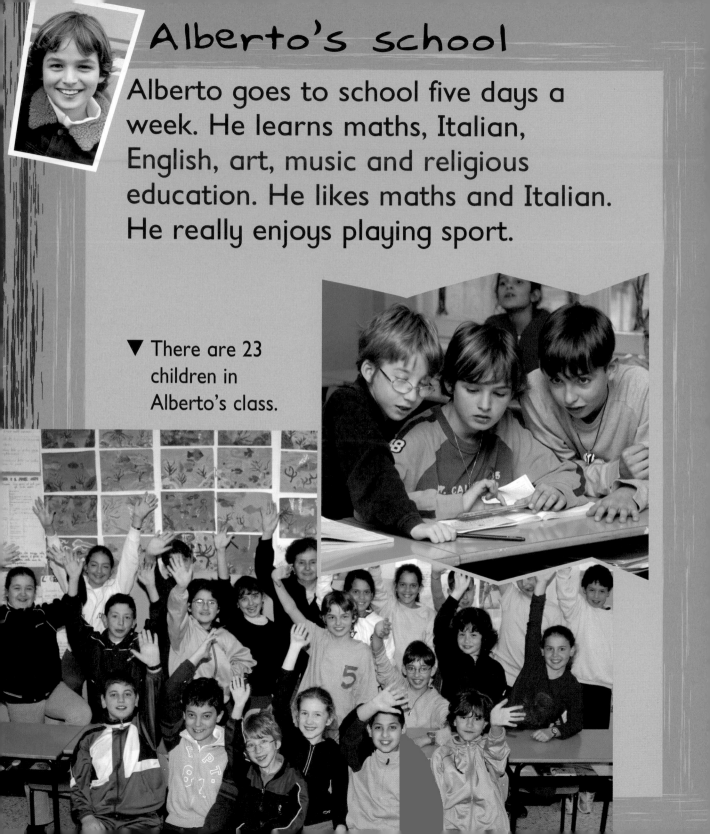

Alberto goes to school five days a week. He learns maths, Italian, English, art, music and religious education. He likes maths and Italian. He really enjoys playing sport.

▼ There are 23 children in Alberto's class.

Alberto has many friends. He likes
talking to Enrico and he plays football
with Lorenzo and Fredrico. His friend
Fabio makes him laugh a lot.

After school

After school, Alberto does his homework. When he has finished, he likes to play football with his friends in the park. Alberto loves playing outside.

▲ Alberto wants to be a footballer when he is older.

26

▼ Alberto sometimes meets his grandmother
when she walks her dog.

Alberto also enjoys swimming and
playing the drums. His grandparents
live nearby, so he sometimes sees
them after school.

Food

Italy is known for its tasty food. The markets sell delicious tomatoes and olives. Pizza and pasta are Italian foods. Today, they are eaten all over the world!

▼ Pizzas are made in special pizza ovens.

▲ Pasta comes in many shapes and colours!

◀ Italy is famous for its ice cream.

Many people enjoy seafood caught in the Mediterranean Sea off Italy. Italy also has many mouth-watering puddings, like **tiramisu**.

Italian fact file

Flag	Capital city	Money

	Rome	Euros

Religion
• Most people in Italy are Roman Catholic Christians. There are also Jews, Muslims and Protestant Christians.

Language
• Italian is the main language of Italy.

Try speaking Italian!
Ciao! .... Hi! (or Bye!)
Come sta? .... How are you?
Grazie.. Thank you.

 Find out more about Italy at
www.heinemannexplore.co.uk

Glossary

ancient something that happened or started a long time ago

architect someone who plans and designs new buildings

canal a waterway built for special boats

earthquake sudden movement of the ground caused by rocks under the earth

gladiator man trained to fight other men or animals, for people to watch

gondola light, flat-bottomed boat with a high point at each end, pushed along by an oar

festival big celebration for a town or country

plain large, flat, grassy area of land with few trees

tiramisu pudding made of sponge cake, coffee, cream, mascarpone cheese and biscuits

traditional something that has been going for a very long time without changing

volcano mountain that has a hole down into the Earth. Sometimes melted rock and ash erupt from it.

More books to read

Around the World: Food, Margaret Hall (Heinemann Library, 2002)

Continents: Europe, Leila Foster and Mary Fox (Heinemann Library, 2002)

What's it like to live in Italy, Jillian Powell (Hodder Wayland, 2003)

Index